I0605222

PRAYER HOLDING NIGHT

Other Books by Lupe Mendez

Why I Am Like Tequila (2019)

PRAYER HOLDING NIGHT: NEW & SELECTED WORKS

by Lupe Mendez

with an Introduction by Jonathon Moody

TCU Press
Fort Worth, Texas

TCU Texas Poet Laureate Series

Library of Congress Cataloging-in-Publication Data

Names: Mendez, Guadalupe, author. | Moody, Jonathan, writer of introduction.
Title: Prayer holding night : new & selected works / Lupe Mendez ; with an introduction by Jonathan Moody.
Other titles: TCU Texas poets laureate series.
Description: Fort Worth, Texas : TCU Press, [2025] | Series: TCU Texas poet laureate series | Summary: "The poems in this collection span a 20 year writing career (2005 - 2025) in which Mendez has worked to speak on issues and everyday experiences. The poems here cover his view on travel and art, historical events and disasters and even a response to Texas politics with a series of never before seen blackout poems. Mendez began his career as a performance poet, cutting his teeth on stages near and far across the Texas landscape and these poems capture all the moments with care and understanding"-- Provided by publisher.
Identifiers: LCCN 2025014687 | ISBN 9780875659282 (hardback)
Subjects: LCSH: Hispanic Americans--Texas--Poetry. | Texas--Race relations--Poetry. | LCGFT: Political poetry. | Erasure poetry.
Classification: LCC PS3613.E482283 P73 2025 | DDC 811/.6--dc23/eng/20250404
LC record available at https://lccn.loc.gov/2025014687

TCU Press
TCU BOX 298300
Fort Worth, TX 76129
www.tcupress.com

Designed by Bill Brammer

Dedicated to the memory of Eusebia Mendez Medina,
my mom; to Jasminne and Lucha Mendez, the stars that
guide in my dreams and my every day; to Pedro Mendez Gonzalez,
who has shown me how to hold the earth in my hands.

20

CONTENTS

Image Credit: Ramiro Ramirez

INTRODUCTION

Dear Reader,

What you have in your hands is a prayer that's dipped in Mezcal. A fiery testimony keeping empathy's blood circulating while residing in a messed-up country "where [even] the air runs to hide." In Lupe Mendez's *A Prayer Holding Night*, you're invited to witness the lives of padres, madres, husbands, wives, migrants, and maestros who're battling everything from Anti-Brownness to Homeland Security.

With the first section entitled "The New Ones," you'll find Mendez as a confident formalist shaping his voice within the forms of pantoums, villanelles, and contrapuntals. And you're treated to a brilliant series of redacted/blackout poems. It's startling yet powerful to see how the omitted words in statements from Gov. Abbott and Lt. Gov. Dan Patrick mimic the *erasure* that's happening to minorities. It's Orwellian to the tenth degree, this American society where gun legislation takes precedence over human lives, where a politician's insistence on lifting face-mask regulations takes precedence over Dr. Fauci's and the CDC's admonitions.

In the selections from *Why I Am Like Tequila*, it's challenging for the speaker in these poems to find solace in a celestial body (i.e. the crescent moon) and in flesh and bones. Perhaps Mendez is suggesting that the only beauty left is language itself. Spanish. Arabic. Hindi. Languages rolling off the tongues of those whose citizenship status might be questioned. Or is it that beauty lies in the power of introspection as it occurs in "What My Father Really Means," which, of course, is in direct conversation with Langston Hughes's "Mother to Son"?

Beneath the macro-level madness that Americans are subjected to, there's madness happening from within the physical frame in the form of an auto-immune disease or in the form of a miscarriage in the haunting poem "The Reason We Don't Come Over for Your Daughter's Birthday." At times, though, all the speaker can do to alleviate the mental and physical strain is to give a back massage. Even if the masseuse's hands don't possess the power of a prayer holding night, there's potential in developing the courage to dream. Of a place where people from "Juarez . . . El Limón . . . [and] Sugarland," can catch a breath.

With all this being said, you'll never look at a "midnight road" in the same way again after having read "Maybe About An Hour." You'll never look at an educator in the same way again after having read "Off Period": a poem in which a teacher listens to his student's anxieties about possibly being deported. But isn't that the power of a poet? Having the ability to enable scholars and non-scholars to build new associations between two unlike things via nuanced comparisons?

There's so much more commentary that I'd love to offer, but Lupe Mendez has this on lock—so much so that a nun would buy him shots of tequila.

Deuces,

Jonathan Moody

The New Ones

EL CUERPO AVISA

Todo mi maíz se llevó, ni pa'comer me dejó
El Barzón – Luis Perez Meza

Esas tierras del rincón,
I look at them como un buey pando,
feeling the dry earth, crunch under
my boots.   Es Julio, y si sigue así,
dirán que es sequía.   I pray it is not.
For now, I will do
what we have always done. I will work
like my father él y sus mandados.
En las labores. We will fix a fence,
the barbed wire, cut, retwist, cut,
retwist until a new post is put in place.

Levantamos rostros al ver las nubes,
all gray, completamente llenos de agua,
but it isn't meant for our hectares.

Quizás mañana mijo.

He looks at me.   He says,
vente, algo rapidito.   We go
into the fields. Rows of little milpitas
all around us. I know what we must do.
We must bend over, pull up the weeds,
all the milpitas that are growing wild,
arrácan viejo, my father says. I have canas.
And a belly.   But my body remembers.
Esta tierra. This land,   these hileras.
48 hileras to traverse, mano over mano –
pull everything that does not follow the rows.

It takes us over an hour. We laugh.
I remember the feel dry earth
in my clutches. The clump of green
entre mis dedos, dusting
the roots on the thighs of my pants,
returning soil to soil.
This would been done in 30 minutes
if I was a kid. I would have earned 5 pesos
and a Pepsi.

Hey, I say, *me duele la espalda.*
My father laughs and says
something about his rodillas. But we do.
We pick the 2 hectáreas clean. We talk
about how much my aunt will make
from this cosecha de elote. Suficiente
para pagarle a alguien más joven
que puede arrancar esta jodida yerba.

Vámonos mijo
- *que esta yunta ya ni anda.*

URGENT TELEGRAM ASKING MY ABUELO FOR HIS CAZANGA

after Kevin Young

HOLA PADRE ALTO

PRIMO KIKO TELLS ME THAT YOU ARE BLIND STOP SAID
THAT YOU SPENT THE LAST DAY IN APRIL EN LAS LABORES
STOP WORKING WITH YOUR TALACHE YOUR CAZANGA

STOP SAYS YOU USED THE TALACHE AND STRUCK A ROCK
SPARKS FLEW INTO YOUR HAZEL EYES NOW YOU CANNOT
SEE STOP SAYS YOUR EYES ARE ALWAYS IN PAIN STOP

MIRE PADRE STOP I WANT TO BE ABLE TO GO HOME
HELP YOU STOP MY HANDS ARE AS GOOD AS HIS STOP
I WILL WORK UNTIL MY BODY GIVES OUT STOP BUT

I AM ONLY GOOD WITH THE WORDS STOP I FORGOT
HOW TO FETCH AGUA DEL POSO STOP HOW TO DRINK
CERVEZA WITH THE MEN AFTER THE DAY HAS ENDED

STOP TEACH ME A BIT MORE STOP SEND ME THE CAZANGA
STOP LA CAZANGA STOP SO THAT I CAN PRACTICE SWINGS
HERE IN MY YARD STOP MAYBE BEHEAD A FEW PUMPKINS

BEFORE WINTER IS OVER STOP PERHAPS WE CAN TALK
BY PHONE STOP MAYBE HAVE MORE THAN A FEW KIND
WORDS FOR EACH OTHER STOP DON'T FEEL YOU HAVE

TO STOP I NEVER MEANT TO LEAVE YOU STOP BUT
THE WORLD IS BIGGER THAN THE CERROS THE STARS STOP
I KEEP DREAMING OF COMING HOME STOP MADRE SAYS

YOU TALK ABOUT ME IN YOUR SUEÑOS STOP
I HOPE YOU DO NOT STOP STOP

MAYBE ABOUT AN HOUR

after Gilberto Alcocer came to the baile, he told everyone
the pizza place in Arandas was the best. Said, "*I will take you*

if you bring pretty girls and cerveza" -he left people standing,
mouths open, managed to greet all the sweet girls, seated

along the back wall in the party hall, "*¿Qué me cuentan, bonitas?*"
Besó el nectar, cada muñeca, lamió sus labios, y después,

not a swig missed, Mezcal drunk, drove dizzy on a midnight road
into a family, mándandolos al diablo—todos a tocar un corridor

por la carretera noventa. He lost a leg that night,
his father would not see him, el monte shook its head, "*Qué triste.*"

My tío, who drank with him the night of the baile, laughed
when Gil pissed his pants, watched him drive away,

went to confession. He said a prayer, a "*Dios te salve, Maria,*"
but forgot the rest. He could not sleep for days. His mouth was dry

in the dirt, cracked, and did not speak. He visited Alcocer in prison.
Gil, in a wheelchair, talked, traded stories, good nights in the fields,

the number of mazorcas acumuladas en sacos de arpillera,
the same number, stolen hearts they left across the border, the fist

fights in afternoons for fun, but not a word about the wreck,
not a word about the women they mistreated, the children

they left with empty bellies. They traded palabras inventadas to hoist
each others' spirits, damp scraps, up above the prison walls, let them

dry out on the roof, where the guilt could be washed out by the rain, the sun, the rain, the sun, and a handshake.

At the end of all the glass-wall talks, my uncle remembered another part of the prayer, he said, "*El Señor es contigo*."

WE GOT THIS (A PANTOUM PARA EMILIANO)

Emiliano Herrera III, ¡PRESENTE!
February 17, 1983 – March 27, 2023

With love and gratitude to those I am honored to call my tribe.
I AM because we are.
As a young kid, I was in constant marvel of everything
I learned from my parents, brothers, and sisters.

I AM because we are.
As a young man, I challenged authority
I learned from my parents, brothers, and sisters,
and questioned everything.

As a young man, I challenged authority
As a father and a husband, I've learned so much,
and question everything.
My word for many years has been obedience.

As a father and a husband, I've learned so much,
I have never questioned that God has always loved me
My word for many years has been obedience,
and he has a plan for my life.

I have never questioned that God has always loved me,
I still don't question it.
He has a plan for my life.
I don't always understand, but I believe.

I still don't question it.
Take care of one another.
I don't always understand, but I believe:
If it's one thing that I've learned is that suffering brings us together.

Take care of one another.
I do not feel alone
If it's one thing I've learned, suffering brings us together,
and we will get through this together.

I do not feel alone.
God in me.
We get through this together.
God through me.

God in me.
God around me.
God through me.
We got this.

WHAT A BACKRUB MEANS

My wife suffers an auto–immune bother,
maybe two. This night, I will take a moment
and be a good machista, assuage her, her tender bones
and muscles. I will do them no harm, massage her
to slumber. This is now standard practice.
I don't take too long. I will find all the knots
in her shoulder blades, massage the stress in her
lower back. She carries her tension in her hips.
She will groan, jerk, and finally drift off to sleep.
I know why I am confident with my hands.

I have spent the same amount of time with apá,
when I was younger, with smaller hands, more elbow.
The smell of cerveza and Winston cigarettes stuck
to the pads of fingers back then. My father did not care,
did not speak to me when he got his backrubs.
He wanted drunk sleep. It was hard to watch myself.
I dared not let my nose, my lip, bleed on his back.
It would make him restless. *It took energy*, I thought,
to come after me the way he would. To tear at me.
But in the end, I gained control, could make the man
fall away under my hands.

I did not have to be delicate as I have to be now. No one
attacks me now. No one will press the back of a fist or
a wall against my person. Now I caress the body,
smell the whips of jasmine in the softs of her skin.
I take my time now. My hands covering that much back,
much more than what I could on my father's back. But
I am just like him, I think, a bit heavy handed.

HERE IS WHAT I WANTED TO TELL YOU (A PALINDROME)

I always see all the colors of a reboso flare
out in the air – such bitter navy air
mi madre lets out a llanto – mi Luciano se ha ido
in the dark, sitting over lagrimitas,
we imagine a white luna watches us, breathes
a brisa, watches us in espera, watches us
lleno de espinas y canto – estamos cubiertos de fracaso,
covered in light, we don't say the name of the sun,
because the day would end without you.

Where are you now?

I know why your seat is an empty moment,
I know I could write you a letter, querido padre, but you,
you are still so busy working since childhood,
you didn't finish school, long ago and now,
we fill notebooks for you with words for you,
odes to you, rants to you, wishes for you,
I see all the colors of a rebosa
flame out in the horno – mi madre throwing away
all the things you bought her,
and again, we grow still, making meals
we use the money you send,

but I would trade every cent to hear you,
ask you what the sky looks like where you are,
I want to ask you what the coffee tastes like,
listen to a song, the sounds of a different tongue.
Please take me with you, please go to the sea, touch sand,
touch a cloud, hold a grillo in your hand,
mi madre loves it when it rains, loves all the mirasoles,
all the cempaxochitl, all the tulipanes, hold them
if you find flowers, press them in

the folds of your clothes, save a flower for yourself.
You are dreaming the same moment I wake up.

Where have you been?

I see the threads in a reboso, when you met madre,
the sound of your shoes on cobble stone,
the trees as they make way for you, for your return.
I sit on obsidian rock waiting
for a moment to share a warm embrace,
a song, a hot meal, and nothing more.

Where are you going?

WHAT A BREAK UP LOOKS LIKE (CUANDO TRONARON)

A ten-year-old peeks keyhole curiosities, sees
appendages blur past his bedtime. He asks his apá

why is Tío Reymundo living with us now?

And now Tío has moved into his room, has different
ladies visit, won't go home, warm, with Tía Gloria.
Tells his apá, *sleeping on the sofa is fine*, knows
what a woman is now, naked, her chi-chis uncovered,
can't slumber with all the noises at night, sees the ladies
(none of them remind him of Tía), spend the night.
They never hello or goodbye. He is confused when
Tía Gloria called the house, the ten-year-old picks up
the phone and says hi and Tía says,

listen bitch, I'm not talking to you, put Reymundo on.

Amá takes the phone, tells her not to call the house
any more. The ten-year-old cries says *I am sorry*.

Wonders if tío's golozo plate is as empty as his plática.

CEDEÑO (10.02.02)

No sé si escuchaste los susurros del coro,
o las lágrimas de tú madre, no fueron muchas.
Tu hermano creció tanto, por un instante,

pensé que te vi.

Dijo el sacerdote algo de tragedia y solitud –
que van par en par. Uno nunca sabe cuando
La mano de Dios

te salve de esta vida. Yo sé que te fuiste
en maromas y amor. Vi a tu hijo.

Se parece a tu esposa. Tiene tú carácter,
hablando con el viento, comodo entre la gente,
riéndose de todo.

Alguien le tendrá que decir del hombresote,
el honesto, el humilde que era su padre.

No sé si tengo la fuerza - ni siquiera, el derecho.

Hablando de padres, el tuyo, habló
una obra de ti. Acabó con un hecho en los ojos.
Su voz gatillo con decir:

los días antes del despido de José
eran a la parrilla, quemando hasta el sol.

Pero ese día, del entierro,   del despido,
había una brisa nubes cándidas;

es evidencia

dijo la voz de tu padre,

de que mi'jo siempre iba a cambiar al mundo.

HOW POEMS COME OUT

"You don't understand me, so why do you judge my life?"
- You Don't Know Me, Armand van Helden fea. Duane Harden

There might be a moment, perhaps a Thursday,
most likely a Tuesday, when there is silence in the
joint,
the cinder block walls offer the perfect shallow, enough

to eat the sound of a pencil curving on unruly paper,
you will want to write about how the weather changed
without you looking at a leaf that falls just as you are
staring

at the bead of water, at a string of clouds. Useless
things

for now. This will be your preference, to sit on a rug,
in the middle of the living room, and turn on all the lights,

the accumulated IKEA lamps, in the four corners,
you live in a mid-town apartment, there are no light fixtures
in the center of the room, with brown carpet.

Brown. And you have never vacuumed. You grapple with quiet,
you are waiting, tap the pencil on the paper, follow some
beat

you heard in the last few days. You are hooked. It is a night
time

ritual. You stuck on some magical shit, on some beat, a charge
mixed in with a shuffle of Sade and Armand van Helden,
Acid Trax and Cleptomaniacs. You cannot write in the quiet

hours. They do not exist –
you live with DJs, and you party

with the DJs and that is not a lifestyle,
rather a mission, travel,
carrying cords and mixers,
you live the life of a roadie

– the black lights
cup the corners of your corneas

and you know that fifty forty-fives fit
in one milk crate, the night of a rave,

you will most likely hold up
in a broke down old dance hall or

a warehouse, you will dance away
the night, into sunlight, you will

take breaks to drink some concoction,
fuck standing up out back
to catch your breath, sit afterwards,
watching all the dancers flapping

around in Jncos. But that is not now.
Perhaps it is a Monday.
You'll wait for a DJ to get home,
when the DJ shows up, he will

bring in a new record or
bring a friend and he will
be a DJ too and you will no longer have
worry about one set of turn tables

wires and LP wrappers,
it is a Friday afternoon – help

install the next set of mixers,
subwoofers, surge protectors and not

sleep normal sleep,   dream of normal things, but dream
of dance floors and beaches, glow sticks   ice sculptures, abandoned offices,
all these bass notes, and finally, write   words will pulse in your fingers,

twitch a scribble that lives in your chest,   and should always be on the page.

HOSTIA

Y cuando llegó la hora, se puso a la mesa, y los apóstoles con Él.
Díjoles entonces: "De todo corazón he deseado comer
esta pascua con vosotros antes de sufrir.
Porque os digo que Yo no la volveré a comer hasta que
ella tenga su plena realización en el reino de Dios".
-El evangelio según San Lucas, 22:14-16

I walked in, into a shop. Pristine walls, concrete
floors cornered me. There were chalkboards,
greeting words, with menu items, coffees and sweet
things I have never heard of. I stopped in. It was
cold, it was rainy, and this place, though filled with
voices, was still empty, these tables hollow,
seats with fingers updating status. This coffee house,
industrial, old, gutted, cold. I smelled food, this place
had a page full of food, but did not feed. No one
looked up. No one looked out through large windows,
oh my Houston, the skyline, the raw. There was a line
outside. I bought what I could buy, ran fast into
a food line. Right across the street, filled with voices,
filled with laughter, filled with the hungry. I smelled
the bread, smelled the chicken broth, saw eyes seeing
me, the tension of law breaking–the city tickets you
for things like this. Don't be hungry or be homeless.
Never give food. I broke the law. Gave this lady a few
cake balls and cavities. I think I gave her cavities.
And she said it was the best bellyache she ever had.
Heard a man say this was better than eating alone
in his unit with no lights. And I remembered you.

Remembered when we scrounged around for change,
ate one hot meal between the two of us, in the dark.

We ate salado, agridulce, ardiente, whole, holy, fuller,
discípulo, santa, reina, warm, light, unbroken, rich,
deity, the good, more human. This is how we soul.

Eat of my meal, of my words, eat my wishes and pray,

you don't turn into a lavish Toutsuit on an "EaDo"
corner Commerce and Chartres. I've asked if they donate
uneaten breads, they don't. Too busied cutting mint
to dress a cupcake, with watering mouths across the way.

A POEM FOR JANIS SCOTT

I read the article about you,
about your passing.
Santa Janis de los camiones
San Janis de las guaguas,
You always riding to every
art show, every reading,
You see us children, us
fumbling, making mess.
I see your face on my screen,
I see your face in the crowd
at Inprint readings.
at Brazos Bookstore readings,
at readings at MECA,
at Nuestra Palabra readings,
You are always there.
You have been here so long,
I put you in a poem
many years ago,
you are a blessing.
My heart is a little broken,
always a smile on your face,
always a warm handshake
and a thank you. I remember
once I said no, no, thank you
you said, *oh I love this,*
keep going, keep going.
Is it crazy that I look for you
in crowds when I read?
I know I'm in the right place
if you are there.
I know you are here.
I am doing something right
if I see you in the audience,

you wrapped up in a shawl,
smiling in some seat.
I think I will always choose
to see you, remember you.
No, No, thank you.
Thank you for coming,
Thank you for seeing us all.

HYMN OF THE DOUBLE SHIFT WORKER (A VILLANELLE)

Ánimo, hermano, there are no early morning breaks,
you have to stay up on the charge, froth up, around,
lunge a bit forward, sweat big, see what the day makes,

take the surface of the earth, warm in finger aches,
work does that much, keeps the joints quite bound,
ánimo, hermano, there are no early morning breaks,

just the sound of fullness in the air, breath that fakes
at first, a stumble when you rise, keep up, don't drown,
lunge a bit forward, sweat big, see what the day makes.

There might be a time when you get the shakes,
But hustle in the ruckus, shake the tired down,
Ánimo, hermano, there are no early morning breaks.

Don't talk about all the tired in you that puts on brakes,
Build that into a knot, a silk one, that flutters underground,
Go 'head, lunge a bit big, see what the day makes,

There is no choice, that little money come down in flakes,
food must fill the belly, lights have to work, the pulse pound,
In the eyes of your dear, peace, home, it's a prayer that shakes,
so get some ánimo, brother, there are no early morning breaks.

LAS GOLONDRINAS

"que me toquen las golondrinas, que en sus notas lleven a mi alma"
- Tomás Méndez

The breeze picks up,
catches the moon,
right as she reaches out,
rattles a Tamarindo. I do not
want to leave. I walked
around the barrio,
a gas lamp lights
the street,
no shadows,
merely footfalls,
the ones I make,
in the distance.
I linger a bit,
golondrinas dart around me,
whisper
You can stay.

They'll build me a nest,
en el quiosco
dentro de la Plaza al lado de San Miguel Arcángel,
where the voices emerge,
at the corners of windowsills.

Still.
They always sing,
at the tinge of wind,
at the sound of a busy day ending,
a cacophony-filled dusk, settles
over the cobblestone, the sound of a pen,
dipped in

a tintero,
every night, a story,
written once,
read a million times a day.
So I chose to stay,
a new golondrina, resting, on a roof tile,
above this other home, no.
Home.

A LIGHTHOUSE CAN BE SOMEONE'S HOME ON FIRE

Ike's quiet eye shifts a little to the left, hiding
the second half of his fury. Goddamn fever sweats.

Ike is an angry, stubborn boy, a devil
messes with you right as you dark slumber.

For a moment, a few of you can take a breath.
In the middle of the water,

this is your chance;

now the sky is blue calm,

go ahead

take a peek.

Outside in the cold, the dank, the deep,

it is the same as inside. There is sand and sea
water everywhere. There is always water

here. We have always seen this before. No
sidewalks, no grass, no cars, no gardens

survive. Only a few houses stand,
or the leftover stilts, lone towers high

in sun. Some have collapsed under the weight –
rain and worry. You know this won't last long.

Go quickly.

Ike will lurch forward soon. He is starting to surge.
You should grab what you can; pray the wind won't
hurt, ignore the last house on the left.

It's on fire.

You don't need to go see, knock on doors,
see if Henrietta or Carla, Alicia or Allison got out.

They were stubborn,
probably slept as lightning struck.

You know the ships could use their home now,
an instant lighthouse in a sea of grey water.

The smell of burnt wire and black smoke will
billow orange puffs, don't stare too hard,

a lighthouse, then, can be someone's home.

AN EXTROVERT WATCHING 45'S CORONAVIRUS ~~BRIEFING~~ LOCURA (A PANTOUM)

Ese viejo anaranjando suggested injecting disinfectants
as a treatment. "Maybe you can, maybe you can't . . .
I'm not a doctor. But I'm, like, a person that has a good
you-know-what," he said, pointing to his head.

As a treatment, maybe he can, maybe keep quiet.
And we stare at the screen, a bit of a rage in the throat,
try to remember you-know-what, and point to our heads,
every night grows brighter, full of people waiting on healing.

And we stare at the TV, a bit of alone in the room
perhaps we should picture each other, all lit up inside
every night grows brighter, full of people waiting on light.
Let's ingest each other's words, una cena bien sana, sana.

Perhaps we should draw pictures of each other, light inside.
We can write each other letters or postcards or just talk.
Let's digest each other's words, una cena bien sana, sana.
Let's meet in an open field, shout secrets and Lotería.

We can send each other letters or incantations or just dream.
It would be good to see you again, perhaps full of moon light.
Let's meet in an open field, shout secrets and el buen chisme.
I'm sometimes alone, I'm a person, pointing to my hot heart.

MORSEL (On Goya's *Saturno*)

I am hungry, mi'jito. Siempre
estoy muerto de hambre. I'm hangry,
mi'jita. Busco algo, a need to sink
my teeth into something hunted.
Tu madre, Ops, doesn't see it this way,
says I should slow down. Take a meal
with family in daylight. Enjoy company.
A meal is better at the table. But
something me molesta, gnaws at me,
a dream I had. You children laugh
at my grave. You squatting a piss
on my headstone, you, laugh at the dead
roses on stone. All that remains of me,
a statue, a sixth day of the week honor.
My name. A goddamn day. Despierto.
You are little now. Plump, ripe, supple.
You are full of fats. Tal vez tu madre tiene
razon, I should have my family for a meal.
This will warm me inside, to have you,
close to my lips, close to my heart. Draw
strength from your eternal tierno touch.

GOVERNOR ABBOTT DOES NOT CARE ABOUT YOU

We need to erect a complete barrier
against any government official
anywhere from treading on gun
rights in Texas.

Anyone who shoots his grandmother
in the face, has to have evil in his heart.

As long as I am governor of Texas,
your right to keep and bear arms
will never be infringed.

It could've been worse.

We passed open carry and campus
carry. People said it's going
to be the O.K. Corral.

None of that happened.

I have signed more than 20 laws
to protect your 2nd Amendment rights.

And so, I don't think

there is going to be any bad side effect to it.

We have god-given rights.

god, guns and greg,

that is what Texas stands for.

LT. GOV. DAN PATRICK: STATEMENT ON FORMING THE SENATE SPECIAL COMMITTEE TO PROTECT ALL TEXANS

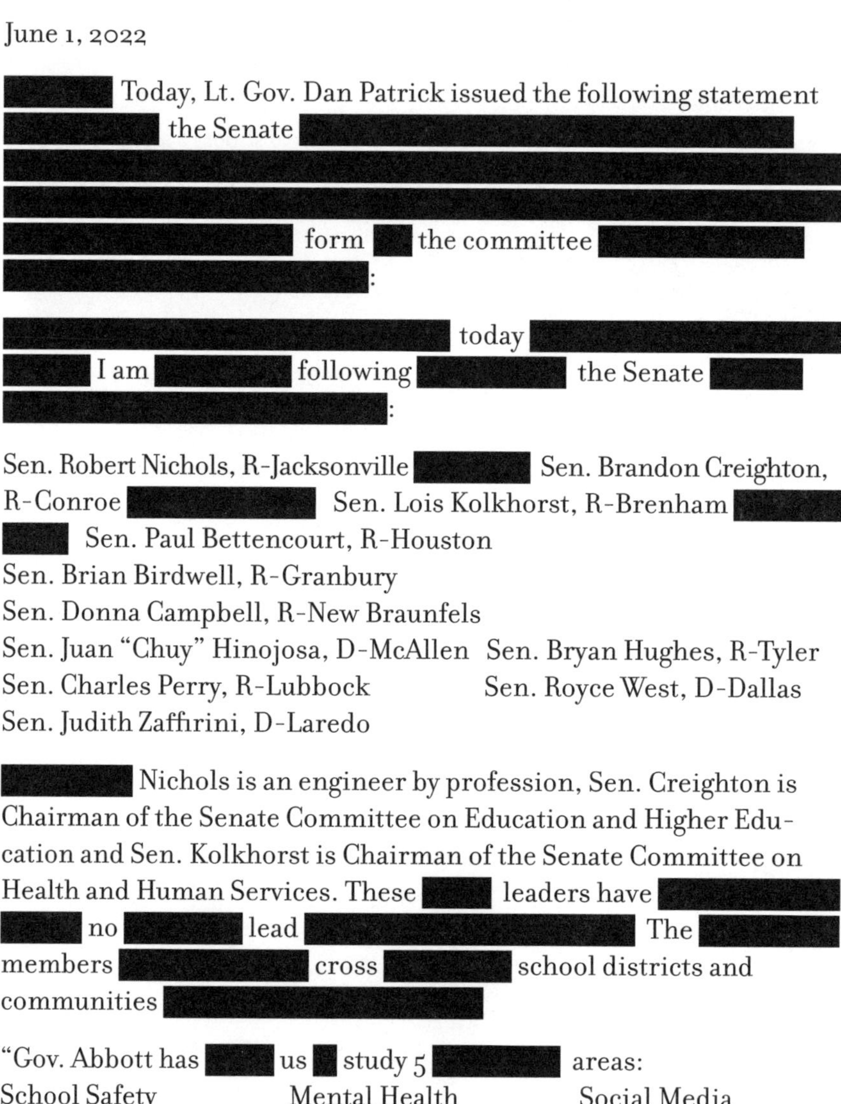

June 1, 2022

Today, Lt. Gov. Dan Patrick issued the following statement
the Senate
form the committee
:

today
I am following the Senate
:

Sen. Robert Nichols, R-Jacksonville Sen. Brandon Creighton, R-Conroe Sen. Lois Kolkhorst, R-Brenham
Sen. Paul Bettencourt, R-Houston
Sen. Brian Birdwell, R-Granbury
Sen. Donna Campbell, R-New Braunfels
Sen. Juan "Chuy" Hinojosa, D-McAllen Sen. Bryan Hughes, R-Tyler
Sen. Charles Perry, R-Lubbock Sen. Royce West, D-Dallas
Sen. Judith Zaffirini, D-Laredo

Nichols is an engineer by profession, Sen. Creighton is Chairman of the Senate Committee on Education and Higher Education and Sen. Kolkhorst is Chairman of the Senate Committee on Health and Human Services. These leaders have
no lead The
members cross school districts and communities

"Gov. Abbott has us study 5 areas:

School Safety Mental Health Social Media
Police Training Firearm Safety

“I hold hearing
I give the families of
Uvalde time to complete all funeral services before beginning
wish I have
the House

here

We will work with
Crime

“All of us working together is politics.
It is about doing all we can see another tragedy
like this happen again in Texas

LT. GOV. DAN PATRICK: ONE THING WE CAN DO RIGHT NOW TO BETTER PROTECT OUR STUDENTS BEFORE A NEW SCHOOL YEAR BEGINS

June 3, 2022

HOUSTON – Today, Lt. Gov. Dan Patrick issued the following statement:

" there will be school shootings in the future. there is one thing we can begin to do right now without waiting

every member of law enforcement across the state, approximately 80,000 officers, respond to an active shooter Of course, more training is needed, we wait for another school year -equip our police

"I am asking in a budget to begin buying bulletproof shields so every member of school law enforcement has one.

"This will bullet-proof shields to all law enforcement. We have used transfer authority this year to spend billions on the border. We can surely find this amount of money to better protect ~~our kids~~.

every school district officer we can rest at the front of the line

across as many of our nearly 9,000 school campuses before the fall.

all responding law enforcement live

to take quick action

LT. GOV. DAN PATRICK: STATEMENT CELEBRATING U.S. SUPREME COURT'S DOBBS V. JACKSON WOMEN'S HEALTH ORGANIZATION RULING

June 24, 2022

Lt. Gov. Dan Patrick issued this statement today

"Today is a tremendous day for

evil

in our state.

I first took office in 2007, my top priority.

the Sonogram Law, and in 2021,

the Heartbeat Act, which dramatically

reduced

justice. The left will surely

fight in Texas

ruling

a human life

is not a victory for all of

humanity.

OPERATION LONE STAR BRINGS NATIONAL ATTENTION TO GROWING BORDER CRISIS

September 2, 2022 | Austin, Texas | Press Release

Governor Greg Abbott, the Texas Department of Public Safety (DPS), and the Texas National Guard work together to stop people in Texas, and between

migrant apprehensions and this border

Texas has also a busing mission providing

dangerous gaps Every individual who would have otherwise made their way into communities across Texas and the nation

GOVERNOR ABBOTT ANNOUNCES MIGRANT BUS ARRIVALS AT BORDER CZAR HARRIS' RESIDENCE IN WASHINGTON D.C.

September 15, 2022 | Austin, Texas | Press Release

Governor Greg Abbott today announced the two buses of migrants from Texas outside the United States Naval Observatory in Washington, D.C. early this morning. The buses dropped off over 100 migrants from Colombia, Cuba, Guyana, Nicaragua, Panama, and Venezuela.

he continues ignoring and denying the crisis endangered and overwhelmed communities for years Governor Abbott. has yet to even see firsthand the impact of policies he has helped implement, he will continue sending migrants to cities like Washington, D.C.

This arrival of migrants comes days after he claimed the southern border was a border crisis. This busing is part of the state's ongoing response reckless border policies that are overwhelming

Governor Abbott

PAXTON SECURES ANOTHER MAJOR VICTORY AGAINST BIDEN ADMINISTRATION, STOPPING THEIR ATTEMPTS TO FORCE WOKE GENDER POLICY ON TEXANS

October 6, 2022

Attorney General Paxton has another

ruling in favor of halting
rules.
The decision

to adopt rules
based on sex.
Texas Agriculture Commissioner Sid Miller supported this
and provided conflict with
reason
Paxton later

threatening to cut

safety and protection of Texas children
Paxton attempts

to push back against the law

PAXTON ONCE AGAIN VICTORIOUS IN FEDERAL COURT AFTER SUING TO END FEDS' UNLAWFUL DACA POLICY

October 13, 2022

I applaud DACA as unlawful
said Attorney General Paxton. " chaos
is our communities and
our border
now."

GOVERNOR ABBOTT DIRECTS TEA, SUPERINTENDENTS TO PROHIBIT COVID-19 VACCINE MANDATES FOR STUDENTS

November 17, 2022

Governor Greg Abbott today directed the Texas Education Agency
(TEA) and Texas school superintendents the COVID-19 vaccine
cannot be a part of school

In letters
the
Governor
allows Texas parents to opt out

health care.

"Despite attempts at federal health care decisions
of Americans, in Texas we continue to defend the freedom
of

COVID-19 Texas schools shall
not require students to receive vaccine for any reason."

LT. GOV. DAN PATRICK: STATEMENT ON THE PASSAGE OF SENATE BILL 16 – BANNING CRITICAL RACE THEORY (CRT) IN TEXAS UNIVERSITIES

April 12, 2023

"Last session, we banned kindergarten through 12th grade be taught race, sex, or ethnicity. In 2023 be common the radical drive to divide society

" there was no question we would ban teaching Texas determined to indoctrinate our students with revisionist history, I thank Sen. Hughes and the other Texas Senate Republicans for standing with divisive and ugly practice s."

SB 16, bans teaching of Texas

GOVERNOR ABBOTT STATEMENT ON CRITICAL
SCHOOL CHOICE LEGISLATION

May 14, 2023

AUSTIN - Governor Greg released a statement as the Texas Legislature considers school choice legislation in the final weeks of the legislative session:
choose the
remains this session. A majority of Texans from across the state and from all backgrounds support school . The Senate's version of school makes about 5.5 million students eligible, while the House's version proposed last week would make about 4 million students eligible. The latest House version of school , which came out this weekend, only applies to about 800,000 students. It provides less funding for special education students than the original House version of the Senate bill and denies school to low-income families that may desperately need education for their children. This latest version does little to provide meaningful school ,

this session has progressed, the number of House members supporting school
will be eliminated school choice is attracting
more legislators.

divide Parents and their children My staff and I will continue to work around the clock with the legislature to reach that goal. failure
Parents and their children deserve less."

The Selected Ones

LAYERS

I. Lupillo

I asked apá why this name.
He laughed. *The night you were*
born, your amá almost died,
toxemia in veins, and outside,
the moon was a breeze. He asked

about amá in broken English.
The doctor told my father,
pray – only one will make it.
Tío Chilo once said apá sharpened
glass pieces to shave. I asked,

how did apa not cut himself?
Tio laughed, *muchacho, cada*
hombre se corta. blood is nothing.
Amá said on my born day, she
floated out of body in a red line.

Saw herself, heard a baby coo.
Amá had to have a hysterectomy.
Perhaps age or I broke womb.
The night my apá first crossed Tejas,
he prayed la virgencita would guide

him. He prayed to a breeze, a moon.
I imagine him in prayer the night
I was born, in a capilla. *Querida*
Virgen déjamelos vivos. My body,
my ama's blood pooled in this name.

I've wondered if I am the bestia
he asked for. I have not fought,
howled at the moon like he. I haven't
mixed mud, sweat, the way amá has.
But, I've been lumbre every night.

II. La Negra, La India (La Virgen de Extremadura)

the first man she meets is a doctor/Lucas/dresses her in reds and golds/ says he likes black girls/puts her on a pedestal/asks if she wants to leave Syria/they travel red dirt roads/where the mirasol grows/they come across the caballero Gil/she asks him to build a templo for her/he does/ he dies in the last brick/between the mortar and the fingers

there's a rumor/an Italian with three boats/he wants to sail to some new place/asks her to come along/they sail awhile/she watches the skies/he eats all the granadas the night before landing/yells he plans on staying/the new neighbors don't understand/they mumble between themselves/they bring food/fancy pots/mounds of gold/he answers them/in cut off limbs/in dog chase bites/in ankle shackles/separating babies/ small pox/mixed-up tongues/dead horses

she goes up in the hills/walks a while/meets a poor boy/Juan/asks him to build her a place to stay/says he knows a guy/who knows a guy/who knew the lady that lives here/up the block in Tepeyac/lady eats maize raw/lets the kernels stick to her teeth/talks to deer/has a house of mud/ it was burnt down/still hangs around in the trees/in the mouths of the dying/in the ears of corn

they meet/trade some stars/they embrace/they kiss and stay together/ she gives Juan some roses for his troubles/all the neighbors/they come by/bring candle/bow their heads/raise arms to the sky/sometimes/one of them goes out on the porch/watch as they all talk at once/how they cut the necks of goats/paint the doorways with blood/they ask her to bless some crops or watch over them/like she was going to make flowers appear/like in the snow or something

II. December 12th

My bones lay in,
a river,
a howl at all the blood moons,
the lights,
the candles

in front of an altar, not far away.
I am in the womb in
Tonantzin,
mother of earth,
her son her little
adobe sun, who hides ideas
in stones, washes them
in paints,

paints in lyrics,
in newsprint, draws Catrinas,

in pastles, the color of lasers
in la oscuridad, the color of poverty,
charcoal and rib cages showing
hueso blanco,
waiting to be put to rest.

Soy llanto.
Soy virgen,
un degraciado santo,
a mountain chained to the wind,
a paper treaty, betrayed, moaned,
abandoned.

Soy
José Guadalupe Posada, hungry,

Guadalupe Victoria, victorious,
José Guadalupe Olivares, aka,

a poetry god.

I am La Unión del Pueblo Entero. Punto.

I am

a canine,
a Puertorican songstress,
a Mexican Banda barbaro,
a kick-pusher.

I live

in black volcanic rock
burning, streaming against river,

against the wolves en lo hondo del rio,
in the bottom of the water,

where you can dream in colored light,
dream, dream, dream.
Dream of me.

WHAT MY FATHER REALLY MEANS

I

Si trabajas dos jales y andas de prisa – nomás échate agua caliente en el pelo, los sobacos y enjuaga tu perico y caracoles. [The days will grow into each other, the work hours addict you, the mind falls asleep in upright double shifts, there is nothing wrong with work, with washing your dick in the sink, means you can't miss a minute making money. Clean yourself. Wipe away the tired in hot rags then go back to hustle y trabájale]

II

Al manejar un carro – tu nomás písale mijo, el que se pone encima, atropella al hijo de su rechingada madre.
[You will hear these words said to you: mojado, spic, pocho, americano, wetback, beaner, marijuano, brownie, darkie, alien, illegal, boy, dirty, greaser, roach, rat, flea, anchor baby, de rancho. Ignore the air they float on. Tilt your head toward the yellow of the sun, darker. Grow warmer. Build laugh. Dig, dance, move into the space between these words, these voices, so the only sound heard is a gruñido in their stomachs.]

III

No busques bronca, pero si aparece, mételes un putazo.
[I will be the one to teach you how to fight. You will need to defend yourself from people who disrespect you. I'll pelt fists against your frame. This will be the first memory I place in you: you will drop a Miller High Life from my hands and I will hit your temple, watch you roll down a flight of wooden stairs. You will know the taste of varnished wood lodged in your gums. Smile. We will do this often. Come here and let's begin.]

IV

Méate la mano si te cortas bien mal, luego échate tierra, al rato, tendrás callos bien hechos. [Take care of your hands. You will wash windows and plates and avoid glass in streets. You will remember playing a las escondidas at night, the slice from broken glass as you fall, your hand slick red, palm up – remember the feel of a hot stream from you to wash away a trickle of blood. You will feel the same sting the day you first clean windows. You will have just popped blisters on your palms, submerge your hands into a pail to reach for rags, rush back to that night, piss coating your hand, the sting, the strong smell of ammonia will never leave your nostrils. But your skin will be thicker and those windows will glisten, not a crack among them.]

V

Si se te para ese chilio en los pantalones, guárdalo para tu novia.
[You will find a young girl your age, care for her, you will laugh as you grope and flash body parts, you will flush in the face, blow blood vessels on beach nights, the smell of coconut scented sunblock coating your girl, and you will not have to go to her, with money in your hand, to a room above a bar, a nervous wreck, an exchange of service, an empty physical drive, to fuck with barely a word spoken, the sound of a radiola below her bed, the light scent of sweat and her skin cold, you will never have to know el barrio rojo mijo, because you will know how to talk to women in ways I didn't know they should have been spoken to.]

MANOS (OR PRAYER HOLDING NIGHT)

a fist no
bullets out
the pop of skin
the twist of wrist
where scars pox out
coals rubbed together
where the air runs to hide
first seconds of fresh wound
el significado de un trancazo
gutting a confetti of fish scales
tocando Dos Monedas siempre
the rash that spiders into bleed
reaching out in a pitch so black
gripping collected corn stalks
looking for change in pockets
metal across jawbones biting
bricks against me, against me
combs of warm water in hair
bandages holding paychecks
shovels up in the wet ground
translators when tongue slurs
a shave with a sizzling knife
abriendo ataud sin pésame
age measured in caguamas
red slices to a calf's throat
the nails that scratch white
dotted knuckles magnetic
cold bones on card tables
blisters wrapped in mint
a heart that waits to beat
a shake in the forearms
glass shards in tendons
boxing practice lessons
seconds jabbing reflex
boiled water thrown
thunder up on body
hacksaw for limbs
weighted fingers
axes split roots
the snap of ribs
a flung machete
palms cup clap
tenderness waiting
prayer holding night

MEXICAN ISLAND

I live in forty-five granite rocks in long rows.
This is a pier, a walkway, a moment jettisons
out into the gulf, just past the beach.
The world changes

here. The moon takes care of me.
I am drawn – moonlight,
a brush of sea air,
foam against the jagged that makes this place.

I park one block away. It is always dark
when I walk the Seawall, down the staircase

on 35th St.
I sit just at the edge, where mist collects,
where
bare skin turns sticky salt, where city lights die.

I face the Gulf, the storms, white flashes,
shadows in the grey. Me quito las chanclas
de perdido Stretch toes.
Sand spreads under a midnight foot.

I take a swig of thunder, cheap whiskey,
unos traguitos de mezcal. I have sat with sad eyes.
I will sit with sonrisas, I shall bring my media costilla

here. I confess to the stars. I imagine myself
someplace else. I watch the night change, watch
the tides bruise and break so much, they swell up.

I picture me – thrust myself upon the color horizon.
Jump away into the sea. I will not be able to,
the current along the rocks will drown, rip me.

This is the act – wishing, the act of island, being
at home, longing to be mid air, to be caught
in one large wave – to disappear into some deep.

This is the where the island bends. This jetty, this is
the closest finger into the ocean. I live here. I live.
I hold myself against this want.

SO, HOW ARE YOU FEELING TODAY?

When you say the word/pericardium/I think red/I think viscous/I think fragile/I think full/I don't think puncture/I don't see wound/I don't want to know/you can't breathe right/can't catch a gasp/can't sleep laying down/can't function/you are younger/you take plenty of pills/you have apps on your phone I have to know about/when you fall down/if you fall down/I'm supposed to know/what to do when your fingers turn blue/what to say when they mention renal failure/how to keep a calm demeanor/I tell your parents you are in some ICU/I got the question/ are you taking care of her/I just sigh/I just rub your feet/I just wake you/ don't yell at me/yell at your puto pericardium/that swells up/a three liter coke bottle full of heavy/fluid/ I don't sleep/you don't sleep/when we do/it's two hours/I have bad dreams/about your heart sack/that wraps you up/clings around your lungs/a knot around your heart/that traipses
around a pulse.

You are laying there/wrapped in blankets/wrapped in silver needles/ so calm/your face is lying/I watch your ribs rise/bones expand with a jerk/I hear a click/a thud/a white bone is aching/in your side/I should leave/I should get you a pitcher of ice water/fill your cup runneth over/ lavish you with unbridled rest/you are in pain there/trying not to make a move/make a sound/make a tear fall/stream down a window pane/ looking out into the woods/behind your eyes/in the distance/there are trees/blowing in the gust of wet winds/a few of them/dry and bending/ they expand/they click/twigs inside them break/they grow rigid/they ache/splinters in your heart/it burns.

It's a waiting game/new tubes of blood/the doctors touch you in places I need candles lit to touch you/soft pillows to caress you/the night moon/showing off your hips/your eyes look at me/in a hunger/ hungry for something ripe/you become restless/want to wrap your legs around my heart/you want to bite into my shoulder blades as if they are mangos/you don't want to be here/see it in your eyes/sunken/dark/ you love to hate me/when you are here in the observation room/wires sticking out of your shoulders/out of your breasts/out of your ribs/to get a pulse/to get out of here/you hate me/for bringing you here/to be tested/you teach the pre-med class as they walk in your room/they ask you your history/you show them your heart/in your file/you smile at them/you cry when they leave/you scurry/you fumble around with the tubes/the cords/the drops of tears/the size of stolen bread/quick/dry them away/they might want to study that too.

REQUIEM FOR MY MIJIT@

I am a barrier island, brown
with tepid shores, worries
festering up
in slicks of chapopote

at the bottom of feet.
I am an eye sore.
I tremble at crashing waves,
the boom of thunder.

Déjame solo.
Give me a year or more
to lick my wounds,
to clean my shores,

to address the damage.
We lost the inkling of a baby,
the minute I looked at the moon.
I didn't heed the warnings.

I didn't ransack el tendajo
to prep for this devastation.
I was in awe of the swells
on the jetty. I lost my footing,

the expectation of fatherhood –
Instead, the storm sent
us slowly bleeding,
a hurricane inside the womb.

Nothing looks the same.
We waited for it to take its toll.
I am still waiting.
I am a hungry man,

homeless and in need of shelter.
I remember the day
we told my parents
we were having a baby.

They looked at me
said to *wait and see*.
They are not over their loss, either.
I should have an older someone

to collect sand dollars with,
but they were lost
before my birth.
When my father goes fishing,

my mother looks at the moon,
they are searching for a carita.
They go by night,
tripping on downed palm trees

with a lantern, looking for a child,
lost, little. I should join them,
but I cannot. I am dizzy in sun air.
I bleed salt water onto the road.

I am broken waterlines, uprooted
rip-rap. Forgive me for not wanting
your festivities on my beaches.
I cannot stand the sight –

children, writing names in gritty me.
It is too soon, the breeze off the pier,
too soon for the seagulls to cackle,
too warped to invite you in.

FLIGHT (ON JUNE JORDAN'S "FREE FLIGHT")

There is never enough travel to keep you
home,
a back pack, ready,
rolled up maps, socks, undies,
a vile of holy water, sage in a bag
for the spirits that travel,
that haunt
you too, carry all the ghosts on shoulders, in that bag
filled, crammed with passport forms,
thumb print scans, a room with your shit
laid out on a table, rummage this again,
Mr. TSA Agent, yes, sir,
no, sir, why the gloves?
That's not a liquid,
it's a sensitive skin,
teal colored Gillette eight-ounce gel,
that's not a weapon,
it's a butter knife
for the bread and the decadent, yes,
slick Nutella. Ask him for that.
You have not eaten.
The line is longer
when you get out,
finally,
you are not a terrorist, just checking,
upload all the photos, the blog post,
photo-bomb the shit out of Westminster,
pay three times to get in the Tate Modern,
explode your eyes at the Tate Modern,
over and over and over,
over a pint of Carling
with a pretty Irish girl,
walk her to her place

near Chairing Cross, cross the street, in the puddles,
in the sprinkle, in the gray,   change the gray
to night, dejadaté un momentito en Russell Square-
change clothes, a black Mossimo V-neck
for a heavy polo, fifty percent cotton,
fifty percent, hot,   sweaty,
        walk, you,   you fat ass, walk,
walk, then pack again,   pay the fare, the transfer,
the taxi, to
    get you to Stansted,
the Costa coffee with soy one percent milk,
with a baguette and gouda cheese and a half a Roma tomato,
for a bit,   pop in the plane,   a fifty-dollar flight
for a twenty-pound note,
        fiberglass bus seat
on a plane – no safety instructions,
    no upright tray table,
just buckle your ass in
    or you will slide down the tarmac
in Madrid
        Chicago
            Miami
as soon as you land.   Throw out all the clothes
    you put in the bag,   dip them in Lysol,
dip them in honey,   dip them in boiling water,
get the scent   of exploration   off of them,
get off,
    come on,   you only have another twenty
                minutes,
before she has to leave for her flight,
remember she needs you around
            before you
have to leave for Austin
        Anaheim,
por el amor de Dios,
hurry up and see   you both,   alone,   a sliver of a minute,

don't talk too much, take the sad look
out of your pupil,
you didn't have to leave for so long,
between the rush of conversation –
did you feed the dog
yes
walk the dog
aw fuck
remember to call me
bought you a snow globe in July
Check the dinner,
eat the dinner,
fix the breakfast,
boil the eggs,
pay a bill late
she says she is
late,
try to talk about it when you drop her off
for her next flight hug right,
plan for this new thing, get all tired at home,
rock me to sleep,
sleep,
sleep,
dream,
get up, take a leak,
take a shower, call to say, say goodbye,
forget to say goodbye.
Then, forget the names of the days of the week
or that time changes
or that you forgot to, remember to check
back with her doctor, waiting on the line,
another moment stuck in a line,
a trip,
what a trip,
another minute to see that
no one in this place is going exactly where you are.
Stand still, would you?

A HUMAN RIGHTS WORKER TELLS ME ABOUT THE CUARENTA Y TRES

"Vivos se los llevaron, vivos los queremos"
-rally cry for the 43 missing normalistas

a voice on the other end of a phone ring,
a whisper, checks the door, a look through the blinds,

an ok, no hay nadie aquí –

a breath, a flood of words that reverses blood flow,
the voice on the other end, he, could not let

his tongue slow down, could not let the air
come out of his lungs without llanto

filling the line, the whole room, the whole one
thousand, one hundred and thirty four miles between

there and here – the voice trembles –
there are over one hundred students
there, in the town square, the ones

who come from the mountains – he says, the ones
who want to go back to their homes,

teach Mixtecos how to come out from mountains.
One of them, he's been found, in the moon

light, in the middle of the street, his hands,
dirty from the blood in the puddles, and his face,

not fit for the classroom he wants to teach in,
but a face, a something Posada would have drawn,

a round, pink set of bones, not the skin, not the lips,
but the white cheek, the jaw, the brow exposed

to the evening breeze. This body has been drug
by a car – he says, the police didn't help this

soon-to-be teacher, no, they let him fall in the mud.
Let the face melt away along the brick road. This body,

this boy isn't the only fracaso. He's not the only one
who's missing. The voice on the phone – help me,

gasps for air – help me find

the footprints, the rumors, los ojos, the bus tickets,
los escapularios, the wallets, las fotos, the cell
phones, las huellas, the watches, la voz juvenil,
the shoes, las venas, the breast plates, el aliento
of forty-two more just like him.

Help me,   he whispers,

see if we can find their faces in la selva,
help me see if we can find them   their lives

in the mouth of mayor's wife, tan golosa,
can't lick her fingers fast enough, she can't

even eat all the names at once, without taking
a moment to look around. She doesn't want to be

seen, esa dama, eating the fruit, la cosecha – Ayotzinapa.
But she will eat nonetheless, binge on silent bodies,

until her teeth hide all the limbs, leave only bones,
charred speeches, decay and a rot from such young meat.

A DANCER TELLS ME ABOUT THE CUARENTA Y TRES (PARA CHRISTIAN ALFONSO RODRIGUEZ TELUMBRE)

Y en los suspiros décia él que la seca la llena
-Las Amarillas, Arturo Villela Hernández

It is a hot night when I take the stage, I know
these steps, una lucha para mi, a flutter in the lights,
a flock of birds in my head, a rhythm I cannot step
away from. My home, my Guerrero, suffers a loss,

an absence, cuarenta y tres are missed.

When I look up at the sky – could not see los pajaros
cadernales, I race to put on my dance shoes, to hug
my children, to count the heads in my own classroom,
race to say the names of forty-three sons,

gone somewhere,

engrave them on my dance shoe tacones. I want
a saneamiento, dress up in a huipil, a yellow skirt, a field
full of yellow flowers in my hair. I heard el gavilán say

A mi hijo, le gusta bailar ballet folklórico,

it echoes desde la costa de mi Acapulco,
across the mountains in Ayotzinapa, up this border. I let
the pañuelo flicker around the air, the bird that flows,
buscando respuesta, un nido, un respiro. He came to find

his son, to ask for help, to dance a cumbia with me,
to watch us, came to watch me dance Las Amarillas,
every step was a pounding fight with shadows, the longest
I have ever danced. I can't watch the rostros in the crowd,

feel the tears well up on my face, I keep the beat, close
my eyes every few breaths, look around, think I see el pico
pico, a young normalista, bring his own paliacate and share
a dance with me. It is

an ofrenda, una llamada, an echo, a marcha, a fogata,
a fight, a linterna, una tormenta, a flare, a beckoning, a rezo,
un enjambre, una vibra, a gust, todo los sueños de un pueblo
a pause, un movimiento led with a simple handkerchief.

I make this gavilán, Clemente, cry tonight, hypnotize him
with a bandada that glows, make his heart swell, remind
him of a brilliant picture, a tarima and his son, caught up
in a dance, watch his lips as he mentions   his
son,

all our sons will dance once more.

ANGUSTIA VS. SILENCE

I cannot help you.
you hide inside a cave,
a rock, a mushroom,
won't budge,
someone told you that a woman
is weak or that
that makes everyone
I know, at night,
jerk and moan, you
even touched you, it is
your eye ducts have
a quite birthday party
only five people show up.
It's my fucking house.
and I claim you, my island,
Pop you, you big red balloon
flinch will make you shudder.
will flow right out of you,
brakes against some wall
you to stop running away
out of breath, lost so
those nerves, untangle

the damn things ache so much.
You sit there doing nothing.
I do not think I can help.
gestures, plates brake on
a pot of scalding water

the frame and its door,
minutes, throb, hurts

It is the home of impatience

When you cry
under the dark
you can't even speak
won't share grief
that cries
emotion is a hot blanket
uncomfortable and
when we sleep, I
wince and I haven't
all the corked-up tears
recorded all the falls
every year and
I won't let you in.
I am Ponce de Leon
in the name of grief.
I think
One day all that energy
wildly, will burst. A molotov
up in my insides. I want
from you, end up in a circle,
just sit with me. Let me touch
the veins coiled around
your heart,
I can see it in your silence.
You wear sulk until it stinks.
You don't recognize these
walls, a punch at the ribs,
across my arms, a hand
between
a frozen beer hurts only a few
cracks in a skull. I know these
things.
you live in. I bounce around

on the inside, grow thick skin,
flinging at me, a whirl of grand mal
at my back, a trail of belt buckles
and I bleed. I know when hate
leans, in the door. Drunk. Lost

just like that. Make it intimate.
join this ruckus, the one time,
flex a few screams, don't worry,
At least I know you,

can see fists
seizure strikes
latches on to my lips,
decides where he stands,
in a moment. Get lost
with me,
Throw a few things,
I am used to. Let your body
I can take the hits.
at the end of it all   you will
sleep.

THE LEFTOVERS OF MERMAIDS

When I was a little boy,
My mother would tell me
to jump over the waves

at the beach. This became
some kind of ritual and a game.
I would count how many

I could jump over or
how many I could swim under,
the waves, the salt in it all.

The foams, she would tell me,
are the leftovers of mermaids.
Do not step on them. I can hear her.

Admire the sea, let it embrace you

in slick brown gulf waters.
Dip your cuts, your ulcers,
all those bad sueños, those bruises,

limpliate todo lo sucio,
soak in the waves. Wash away oil
spots in water. Cover up sins,

eat away time in wind and rays.
Inhale summer days that sift in
restless sand, covering sneaky

promiscuous hands.

My mother never mentioned
ulcers, sins, restlessness –

Just the instruction
jump over the waves.

I always imagined the rest
when I was an older boy,

covered in the scent of cocoa butter,
each time a cop would catch

me on the beach with my girl,

uncovering nakedness and sin.
This sea. Perfect, sweet, sin.

DRIVING BY THE OLD STATE THEATER ON AMA'S 79TH BIRTHDAY

She damn near snaps her neck,
eyes stick to the fachada,
an old movie house, bare,
gutted white inside. She smiles,
looks, says,

I know why
you such a bruto, mi'jo.

Unfolds an old memory,
back in Fifty-Eight,
downtown Galveston had signs,
big, stark white-and-black letter signs
Colored here, Colored
there, nothing

para invisibles Mexicanos.

Unknown, unless
you make a mistake –
dangle you in a tree branch
late at night. Rent lady tells me
to be careful at night. Used to
babysit Anita and her pigtails,

a nursing school hustle, a barter.
Anita had a friend,
                    Amá goes on,
beautiful, plump, black, small
Olivia.

Amá loved to teach the girls
how to cook on Saturdays,
pancakes, eggs, eat warm syrup
with a spoon, buy them dolls,
watch them struggle

with time tables and takes them
to the movie house. In front,
it had signs, big, stark white black
letter signs, No Colored
here. *In the building,*

mi'jo, I am bruta, then. Now.

I love Galveston Island winters,
a reason to hide the girls
in my pea coat.
Pay the janitor.
Sneak them through the back door,
their hands warm – sticky
from sweet maple. Their heads

unaware of hate. Their eyes,
their skins are the same in the dark.

THE EXORCIST ON TV THE NIGHT HURRICANE ALICIA FELL

Due to the severe damage, the name "Alicia" was retired in the spring of 1984 by the World Meteorological Organization, and will never be used again for an Atlantic hurricane – it was replaced with "Allison" for the 1989 season. Coincidentally, in 2001 the name "Allison" was retired after striking the same area as Alicia.
- National Hurricane Center, 2010

My family split up that day, my mother, white scrubs, dressed
for her sick-people-in-the-head job, my father, quiet, – watched
black clouds, white flash cracks. The sun hadn't offered a thing.

I couldn't understand the swirls on the screen, the buzz, the ripples,
the arrows that pointed across the TV, but I felt the swoon,
the house swayed with the wind. I smelled sea salt. It made me jerk,

mess up my horse picture, brown, and black with yellow hair.
I heard the seagulls, they laughed as they flew away. I drew them, too,
saw them as they joined the rest of the people in cars and their lights,

those that ran from the water. I told my father I worried
about mother, said she would be home that night. He kept working
in between swigs of Miller High Life and duct tape. I helped him

in the afternoon, x all the windows, between trips to the bar next door.
I prayed for food. I did not eat that day. In the distance, the breaks
in the waves grew tall, throwing up jetty rocks on the roadway, crushed

a man, covered him in granite and sea foam. He didn't even make
a grip when he died. His hand was limp, his wrist was stuck between
asphalt, the glistening rock, the size of the Datsun he was walking
toward.

The smell of fish remained when they pried the piece of jetty off –
he died with a basket full of croakers. He once shined shoes at the
Hotel Galvez, he knew everyone and told my father tales about
old hurricanes

being brutal lovers and about bitter women who found him out in a
cheat. He sat by the waves a lot, taught me how to make paper boats
float in the waves and taught me how to fly kites in storms.

On the TV that night, I watched a white girl whose head spun
around, who spoke in a demon voice, who beat on her mother, threw
a dresser at her, who made the flower filled walls of her house shake,

who made the red stop sign from the corner of the block fly through
our window, made the wind howl with gnarling rain, who made the
door splinter right next to me. The TV blinked black, flung against
the wall,

not a picture moved, but I still heard her laugh, a bit of maple wood
in my arm. The door was gone and out of its space, the lights of the
town emptied. Only the black, only the lanterns and the twigs, the
bushes and the sand,

the colored cars and telephone wires circled overhead, floating in
the breeze.

THE REASON WE DON'T COME OVER FOR YOUR DAUGHTER'S BIRTHDAY

Forgive me, Marlon

is a bittersweet tangerine-sized pill I have to swallow every year.
I hope all the beers, the meals I buy you, friend, keep you
from being angry at me. I cannot eat birthday cake.
A crescent moon sliced at my wife's womb the night
I held my goddaughter, and every year when that girl blows
out a candle, we shudder just a tad, a ruffle in our diaphragms –
another year she celebrates without a play pal, that looks like us.

DYNAMITE

You see that? Yes, I am
all the cafecito freckles collected, all
the birthmarks. I am every costa.
I am sunlight
held in tan dynamite. When I die,
the world tweets, trends on me,
waits for a coroner's report
and even that shit will be a poem.
250 words will break your heart.
When you bury me,
the winds kick up,
so I see all up your skirts, cochinas.
When I was born,
all the languages
yelled out

oh Allah, ojalá, aw hell nah,

– all the cilantro bowed down
before being picked. All the memes
you see online, are the dreams
I cast when synapses snapped
themself against fiber optic cables
my primos planted in rows,
pum, toma – tu cosecha.
I am every grave
found in
Juárez, Sayula, Ayotzinapa,
Querétaro, Mission, El Limón,
La Unión, Villa Grimaldi, Dos Gatos,
Dajabón, Caracas, Jasper, Sugar Land,
the next space, a next space, that next space.
When I wash my face

along a Texas coast,
you drink my aqua-bien-fina.
                                        When I say
we don't work no more, your kitchen
worker stock plummets, you crumble
with wilted translations,
you are at the end of breath.
                                        I hold you up.
                                        I don't ask you
for money.
                                        I vote you off
this puerto, this isla, this canto,
this sueño, this trago, this alma.
I might not let you back in.
Go ahead, get on
the other side of that wall –

you want to live without me
so much, vamos a ver cómo te va.

AN ONLY CHILD

is a raindrop   one that travels
between the ridges of tree bark.
He is fake menopause. She is
unwanted at first. He is born
an accident.

She is on a time clock
from her first breath. He accepts
being   forgotten on his birthday.

An only child

carries their parents   once
they pass away. She asks
too many   questions.
He is always and never alone.   She
doesn't know the world   without

daydreaming. He learns
to look for voices instead of people.
She builds her own brothers and sisters.
He knows how to live and die
      alone before anyone else.

An only child

is a final stock bond blooming
DNA in an IVF hook up.   He
contemplates fucking up
        his pull-out game. She wonders if
the family tree stops at her.

He adapts to scenes – a bruto
transformer at the [insert name of event or venue].
She counts trust as a blade of war.

An only child

is a fighting leon/a surrounded
by hyenas.   He is a barbaro
amongst a room full of laughs. She is most
comfortable/uncomfortable with no one else.
And when
one only child meets another for
the first time,
      they move with caution,   slowly
reading   the eyes,
watching   the hands   to see
if they might have been some related
seeds scattered by a storm or
                                        a strong wind.

OFF PERIOD

para Karen y su padre, Juan Rodriguez

I woke up late the next day, baggy eyes, baggy
hearted, weak and got to sit in my room finally –
with the fluorescents off to hide
from them all, hide from the world,
but it didn't last, because esta niña walks in,
don't worry, she's safe still,
she won't get in trouble, she won't get taken
away – she walks in though, asks
mister can I just sit here
for a second,
a minute, a couple of minutes,
a whole fucking 30 minutes
and I never said yes
and she turns around and madre santa,
she starts with this aguacero down her face,
I want to hug this kid and I do,
and I feel this kid, who breaks
into bits of air in the lungs, breaks down
all her words into sobs, into my arms,
into my veins, and there it is
the fear curled in her lips
that perch the words deportation
and and my dad and he signed into
the INS office and and the men
in green, one of them is the same color
as you mister, the same color as me
means he southern Mexican he probably all
Oaxaca or Nayarit or Michoacán, bronze
and he tells my dad – you gonna be a priority
and my dad, he cries, he shakes,
pleads and cresses his hands and he's all
my daughter, she gonna graduación en junio

and Mr. Oaxaca says, then have your ticket
ready for the day after that and I think like a bus
ticket, like a window seat on a plane,
where he has to fight the air pressure,
ears popping and then fight the pressure
and heart strings popping and I don't say shit,
I rub her back is what I do – you weren't there
to hear her ribs constrict, to listen to her
teeth clink together, to see her eyes blur
into water pools and all I can think of is
when I was 10 and my old man is thrown
on the ground in Falfurias because
he can't get his green card out fast enough
and I jump on the ground with him, cover
his back with my little frame and I get hit
by a billy club and the guy in green is
the same pendejo, Mr. Oaxaca, I think, and
I don't want her to cry any more
and I don't want me to cry any more
and my shoulder remembers
what residency feels like,
what a split family looks like,
what it looks like to see an oak tree,
the tallest, brownest wood cry, so I want
to tell her she gonna be ok because you are
ok and the bell rings,
she owes me an assignment and she says –
they were gonna deport him now and now
I don't want graduation to come, my parents
can't see me cry and my sister can't see me cry
and I get up and I open the window and
I look at this chrome cloud outside, rain filled,
about ready to burst in the distance and I say,
go there, go hide him there,
til I can think of something, til I can build you
a church to sanctuary his ass in, til I can call

up all the Mexica, til I can find all the obsidian
arrows my elders taught me how to make
for that one good battle, til I can figure out
the work I gotta do to save a Mexican and
she says, mister, we Salvi, from La Unión
and I picture an old girlfriend, in a blue sky
with volcanes and Dios and mamones verdes
plucked and solitude and I ask her –
Can you think of a lie you can tell me -
about why you didn't do my reading yesterday?
Mija, tell me anything better than this.

GROWL

He is a 9-year-old artist –
dirty Filas, ripped jeans.
His home is now the school,
draws forever on the walls.

Creates love notes for chiquitas.
Draws the best sol,
captures largatijos at recess,
king of the columpios.

He won't write in words.
Cries when it's his turn
to read from one book,
rips the pages of a novel.

Trades knuckles with bigger
kids behind the dumpster,
for stealing food from plates.
He is lightweight, the fighter.

He would rather do math.
Figures out his hermanitos'
next four bus stops,
dinner and more markers.

Ignores useless adults.
Tells you straight faced.
His papito huffs paint, says –
papá gives me color headaches.

He just keeps drawing.
Smiles. Says it's what feeds him
at night, yet, his stomach,
a skinny long growl at high moon.

WHEN A STUDENT DIES

When you lay there, a brown body floating against
        the edges of a tub, the water warm against
your now cold skin, I hope the last ripples that seep
        into your blood remind you to picture the forest,
the vestments, the wardrobe, the lion's mane,
        and four little white kids you read about days before.
The book, the witch, the rug in my classroom,
        the bookshelf, how check out a book, bookmarks,
the way to turn the page, the way to treat
        a book is the way you hold a child is the way
you should have been held, with your head up,
        your face above the water, not pinned down, no, not
always running from a drunk, run in the fields, hurry,
        defend your life, defend Narnia, live in the back
half of the ropero, escóndete hasta que la noche se amaina.
        Imagine warm nights telling Peter and Edmund about
how you beat back a dragon in your real world – off
        the dark streets of Rampart and Renwick. Let
little Lucy smile at you, tell you to sleep in the grass.
        Look up at the stars, eyes closed, your arms floating
by your sides, the edges of grass against your body.
        Listen to the sound of water in the river next to you,
the rain that drops across your face, water all around as you, lay
        there, lay in there, no longer cold, warm, away from harm.
Live with Mr. Tumnus, mijito, live in the pages, live in Narnia,
        where you can hide forever.

PRAYER OF A WORKHORSE

Oh body, do not corner me,
do not grind me into paycheck,

give me a moment of you, body,
a morsel/laugh/eye contact

give me some time to poet,
some time to scribble moon x 100
blue mark black out page stages.

I teach in a brick box. I am metal,
an insurance horse, don't even have

my own dentist/space/shovel.
When I finally die/cry/dream

someone
will have to find me a substitute.

They will be the only one
who thinks of me –

Where did he put all those things?

And I will have to put myself together,
outside the urn, go back to work,

show them where I put those things,
then ask them if they need help.

I carry around a dead voice vase
full of wind. Wander without me,
body. Let me sleep, sleep, sleep in

for the next few days,
pen a particular pillar, mirror it,

wordsmith the shit wick out long
words, out of short words, a short
work week, maybe that is what is

needed. I cannot depend on you
to hear me. You ask too much already.

You so caught up in you, you only
listen to for the word "you." Funny,
I did write them with you in ~~me~~ mind.

VIOLENT BEFORE THE MOON
(PARA HUITZILOPOCHTLI)

Inside mi madre, I kept blades in my arms
my legs bent, escondí ojos en mis manos.
I imagined what I would say,
what the air felt like. I dreamt people wanted
to touch the sun, but I let the stain of foul
words press against my ears.

Inside I wanted un toque de luz. She let me
know what they said about her, lo que
pensaban de mí, of how quickly I had grown
in her belly, I wrestled within every
floating thought. Esperé tenso, hasta que mi
madre me dejó salir, let me finally face

the audience, with eyes ready to carve me. But
I remembered – mother
said something in a nectar voice –

Huitz, querido mijito, vístete, hold tight to me,
I need you to be ready. Ponte tu mejor traje.

I remembered my sister spat obscenities,
lashing out, how mother was too old to have
four hundred and two mouths to feed.
She called my mother a puta, muchecha, que ni
un dedo tenia para apuntar a la tierra, she, who fooled
around with warriors en el templo, she laughed

at her own magic tricks. She killed mother.
There was no light left in madre, just the blades
I unfurled in my arms. My legs pounced
at my sister, cutting her, threw her beautiful face
her, the moon – then turned to my brothers,

sisters, who looked so vast, made them look
at our mother. Rindieron culto a ella con
un centelleo, con luminiscencia. I made
them the stars. I hid my eyes in the end,
felt the air on my face. I dreamt people

who touched the sun, now the moon, every night.

ACKNOWLEDGEMENTS

The selected poems in this collection have appeared in the listed journals, anthologies or literary magazines in one form or another:

"El cuerpo avisa," *The Common* –Fall, 2023

"So How Are You Feeling Today?" *Luna Luna Literary Journal* – Fall, 2014

"Flight," *Luna Luna Literary Journal* – Winter 2014

"When A Student Dies," *Ostrich Review* – Summer 2015

"A Human Rights Worker Tells Me About the Cuarenta y tres," *The Thing Itself* – Spring, 2015

"A Dancer Tells Me About the Cuarenta y tres," *HeART Journal Online* – Fall, 2015

"Layers," *The New Sound: A Journal of Interdisciplinary Art & Literature* – Fall, 2015

"The Reason We Don't Come Over For Your Daughter's Birthday," *BorderSenses* – Vol. 12, Fall, 2015

"The Exorcist on TV the Night Hurricane Alicia Fell," *Pilgrimage* –Winter, 2016

"Prayer of a Workhorse," *Glass: A Journal of Poetry* – Fall, 2017

"Angustia vs. Silence," *A Dozen Nothing* – Summer, 2018

"Manos (or Prayer Holding Night)," *A Dozen Nothing* – Summer, 2018

The following poems are from the collection – *Why I Am Like Tequila* (Willow Books, 2019), including:

"What My Father Really Means"

"Mexican Island"

"Requiem for My Mijit@"

"The Leftover of Mermaids"

"Driving by the old State Theatre on Ama's 79th Birthday"

"The Exorcist on TV the Night Hurricane Alicia Fell"

"Dynamite"

"An Only Child"

"Off Period"

"Growl"

"Violence Before the Moon (Para Huitzlopchtli)"

MIL GRACIAS

To my partner, Jasminne Mendez, and to my daughter, Luz María—thank you for giving me reasons to dream. Thank you for believing in me.

To TCU Press for doing the good work—supporting Texas poetry and the Texas Poet Laureates who call this place home. Que Diosito me los bendiga.

To you, the reader—some of these poems you might have seen in my first collection, *Why I am Like Tequila*, but the majority of this work is material I have either been tooling over for a while or is absolutely fresh. Thank you for reading, for writing, for caring.

ABOUT THE AUTHOR

Originally from Galveston, Texas, Lupe Mendez (writer/educator/activist) is the author of *Why I Am Like Tequila* (Willow Books, 2019), winner of the 2019 John A. Robertson Award for Best First Book of Poetry from the Texas Institute of Letters. He is the founder of Tintero Projects, which works with emerging Latinx writers and other writers of color in the Texas Gulf Coast region, with Houston as its hub. Lupe earned his master of fine arts from the University of Texas at El Paso, and his work can be seen in print and online formats including the *Kenyon Review*, *Gulf Coast Journal*, the *Texas Review*, the *L.A. Review of Books*, *Split This Rock*, *Poetry Magazine*, and *Poem-A-Day* from the Academy of American Poets. Mendez is the 2022–2023 Texas Poet Laureate.